11 Passive Income Secrets:

How to Stop Dreaming Being Rich and Start Building Positive Cashflow

Phil C. Senior

Table of Contents

Description

If you are tired of working for someone else and according to their rules, then you should read *11 Passive Income Secrets: How to Stop Dreaming Being Rich and Start Building Positive Cashflow*.

This book is a guide to bring you into a life of sovereignty and prosperity. This handbook will bring you the freedom to keep your schedule, make more money than you would have made at your day job, and empowerment where you will achieve greater self-confidence about what you are capable of. This book may just be the start of a brand new direction and a sense of purpose in life for you.

You may find one particular method of passive income generation especially attractive that you will be passionate about. You may see yourself trying out several ways to bring in easy earnings, some of which require minimal extra effort given how seamlessly they piggyback off other methods.

The thing to remember above all else is that if you start small and expand, you will notice the process of transitioning from a 9 to 5 desk job is seamless and easy. Stop believing in the myth that you have to work for the man to have a steady stream of income. Everyone can be an entrepreneur. This book will teach you how you can make a living in a way that is aligned with your hopes and desires.

In this book you will learn the following:

- What passive income is and why it is a better way to make money than traditional active income

- What the benefits of generating passive income are, as well as what the potential risks and things are to consider

- What the in-depth ways of generating passive income are and how to maximize your commissions and earnings

- How to have multiple streams of passive income that come from one source

Introduction

Congratulations on downloading *11 Passive Income Secrets: How to Stop Dreaming Being Rich and Start Building Positive Cashflow* and thank you for doing so.

The following chapters will discuss why it is a good idea to generate passive income and become less reliant on the traditional ways of working. Being able to bring in income during all hours of the day enables you to be free to keep your own schedule and have more sovereignty over your life. If you loathe going to 40+ hours of a weekly day job, you will be thrilled to learn about all the ways on how you can be your own boss by being a passive income generator. Earning passive income is easier than you may think, and you will probably have some (or plenty) of fun doing it.

Before you read this book, you should ask yourself a few questions. Are you fulfilled with your job? Do you feel like you have enough time for yourself? Do you feel creative and inspired with what you do to generate income? Would you be working at the job that you have if you were not financially compensated for it? If the answer to any of these questions is "*No*," then, you will find this book a tremendous help in changing those answers.

There are plenty of books on this subject on the market. Thanks again for choosing this one! Every effort was made to ensure it is full of as much useful information as possible. Please enjoy!

Chapter 1: Generating Passive Income

We all want to feel free. The major step in that direction is financial freedom. Whether we like it or not, modern society is based on money in exchange for goods and services. Money plays an essential role in society—business, education, career, family, etc. This makes many feel incredibly limited in what they can do and what they can achieve. For a long time, it seemed it was by a stroke of luck that somebody was able to leap into financial freedom by either inventing something, discovering something, or having some other fortunate break. Since the rise of the Internet, all of those things have changed.

There are more opportunities today to be your own boss and design your own model for financial sovereignty than ever before. While many work 40 hours a week or even more, all it takes is taking that first step and then another, followed by another, and on and on. You will learn that several of the methods described in this book are easy to start doing. This will surely bring hope to those who wish to escape their menial jobs and do something more in alignment with their passions.

If you are working full-time at a job you hate, you can begin generating enough passive income so that you will be able to switch to working part-time. This will open up a portal to a new reality for you. What this will allow you to do is take an accelerated movement into what is known as the 4-Hour Workweek. This is a concept initially brought into the public consciousness by Timothy Ferris in his book *The 4-Hour Workweek: Escape the 9-5, Live Anywhere, and Join the New Rich*. Frustrated with feeling overworked and burnt out, Tim developed a method of downsizing his energetic output while still being as productive, if not more.

The attainment of passive income follows a similar stream of thought and action. By automating processes that bring about the achievement of monetary gain, you free up your time and energy to do other things. Passive income generation helps you reclaim your energy and become a happier person overall. You will probably not get your workweek down to four hours for some time, but it is possible. Start small. Dream big.

Before we go any further, we should be clear on the difference between passive income and residual income. You may think that these are similar or the same thing, but residual income is quite different.

Passive income, at the most basic definition, is an income that you earn when you are not actively working. The opposite end of the spectrum is active income, which is money that you stop earning once you stop working. Active income is how most people make money and probably how you are generating your income. Active income is perhaps also the reason why you are reading this book so that you can get out of that feeling of enslavement to man.

Passive income will usually require a more significant deal of effort and energy to initiate, but once you get the ball rolling, the ship steers itself. This way of wealth creation brings with it the bonus of making money without putting in any effort. It may take some time before your income generation becomes this automated, but there are success stories all around you. We will look at the specifics later on so you will learn how to begin this journey to financial emancipation practically.

It is important to note that passive income is not a method of wealth creation where you get something from nothing. That is a get-rich-quick scheme; while there are market irregularities that can be exposed, it is not a practical or long-term method of generating income. Generating value for others is the long-term sustainable route, and that is why it is the focus of this book. Creating passive income does take work at first, but you will get to reap the fruits of your labor with minimal effort once that initial momentum gets going.

Residual income is not income at all. It is a calculation of the money you have left over after you deduct monthly expenses. Think of it as your play money. After all your bills are paid, you will hopefully have some leftover money. You can choose to save it, spend it, or invest it. After reading this book, you will probably find yourself doing one or all of these once you step onto the path of passive income generation. Your residual income will likely grow the more successful you become with generating multiple automated streams of income. You will get to live life to the fullest, or at least fuller than you ever have before.

You may have been hesitant about getting involved in passive income generation in the past, but the fact that you are reading this book means that you are now serious about freeing yourself from the old paradigm way of earning a living. It's time to stop worrying whether it will work out because as the great ice hockey philosopher Wayne Gretsky once said, *"You miss 100% of the shots, you don't take."* Even if you do not succeed with every passive income method you take on, you will still succeed. Failure can help pave the way for you to get clear about what you want and learn from your mistakes. You will succeed if you are motivated to live a free life.

Chapter 2: Manifesting Multiple Streams of Income

The traditional way to earn a living is to leave your apartment or house every day and go to work for someone else in their workplace. This typical arrangement involves spending 40 hours or more every week, working for one job, leaving very little time for yourself. If you get to a point where you have had enough, you barely have the time to look for a new job, let alone go into interviews for one. If you lose that one job that takes almost all of your time up in your waking life, you have nothing to fall back on, and you will find your life turned upside down. You may end up becoming depressed and further falling into a downward spiral where it will be difficult to climb out of unscathed.

This doesn't have to be your story. You hold the keys to your destiny. You can become liberated and experience less stress in your life by making the transition into generating passive income. To make this life hack even easier, you should have multiple streams of passive income.

The beauty of multiple money-makers is that, unlike the scenario described earlier, if you lose one income stream, your life is still relatively intact. You may not even need to change anything about your life, such as reducing your expenses. Let's say you are earning $50,000 per year from 5 sources of passive income. If you completely lost one of those sources, which was bringing in $10,000, it would be noticeable, but if you are living in a way where you can save a little bit of money every month, you will be fine for the time being. You will simply find an alternate stream of passive income to replace the one that dried up. This is a more dramatic example of what usually would happen, where you would notice a drawn-out decline in revenue in a failing income stream.

Multiple streams of income provide greater financial security; this is why this book recommends applying several methods to generate passive income. Some of them will be synergistic with others, meaning it will not take that much more effort on your part to open those income streams up. For example, one way to generate passive income is to sell photos you took to websites that sell stock photos. Several companies buy photos to sell as stock images on their websites. You could apply to several of them and get approved hopefully to start selling through a few of them. Sometimes, you will even be able to sell the same photo in more than one stock photo marketplace.

Before we get into the specific ways in which you will be able to create wealth through passive income streams successfully, it is important to mention that your traditional active income job doesn't have to dive entirely into passive income creation. You can go the safe route and start up a small passive income stream while working your normal salary or hourly job and then shift into passive income full-time later on. At first, your passive income may relieve some of the financial pressure you may feel at home. After a while, you may realize that you would be able to live off of your passive income alone.

There is one more thing that you should reflect on before setting up passive income streams. Once you set them up and are earning enough to cover all your living expenses, then what? Do you have an idea of what you would do with your time? Will you be fulfilled and happy doing that for years into the future? What can make this foreseeable circumstance the best it can be? You should write down a statement of intention for yourself; write down what you would do with your time if your passive income covers all your expenses.

Let what you wrote sit for a couple of days, then look at it again. Ask yourself if you would be thrilled about spending your time if you are financially free in the way you wrote it down. If you feel out of alignment with it, rewrite your statement of intention. You may have to repeat this process a few times until you get very clear as to the answer.

It is important to understand that if you are using the lack of money today as an excuse for why you are not self-actualizing, then you will continue making excuses once you have financial abundance. The only difference is that excuses will change, but they will be excuses nonetheless. If you find yourself falling into a pattern of avoiding the actualization of your passions and interests, then you should start working on changing your relationship with them so that you can attract them into your life.

Take your statement of intention very seriously and focus on manifesting it through manifesting passive income. Start bringing your plans into your life in whatever way is possible in the beginning. If you think you do not have the time to do so, look at what distractions are taking away your time and energy from them. This could be social media, TV, or something else. You can always find and make time for yourself if you are courageous and willing enough to take the big leap.

Now that we have the groundwork laid out, we are going to take an in-depth look into the specific ways in which you can bring in passive income streams that will allow you to quit your day job. Depending on who you are and what your circumstances are, some of these may be easier for you to pursue than others, at least at this point in your life. Find what is the path of least resistance for you and go from there. Align with the methods that line up with your skills and abilities. As with the example earlier with stock photo sites, if you enjoy taking photos with a DSLR camera as a hobby, that would be right up your alley. What you enjoy the most will feel fun for you to do and it will feel more like play than work.

So, let us take a deep dive into how you can create your wealth by jumping into the wonderful world of passive income.

Chapter 3: Affiliate Marketing Tactics

For our first look into specific methods of generating passive income, we will look at the world of affiliate marketing. At the fundamental core of it, affiliate marketing is a method of making money by promoting a product or service. In more specific terms, you are a publisher and earn a commission whenever someone buys something from a website that you have linked to from yours. A commission is a small amount of money you earn as compensation for referring someone that ended up landing a sale for a company selling something. This way of earning a passive income is a prevalent method used by websites and people with sizable social media followings and is something we will explore more deeply.

Companies prefer using affiliate advertising because they only need to spend money when they land a sale. Other methods, such as Pay-Per-Click (PPC) advertising, spend money whenever a certain threshold of clicks is reached. AdSense is an example of a company that does this and another passive income method we will look at greater detail later.

Publishers also prefer affiliate advertising because if they find a product or service that is in alignment with what their website is about, then their earnings can go above and beyond whatever money they would have brought in if they went with a PPC affiliate. You can try out both affiliate methods and compare the earnings, or you could use them side-by-side if they appear to work seamlessly together.

Affiliate marketing works best when an online content publisher is trusted to provide meaningful information for its audience. If your audience believes you as being someone that can give helpful advice and information for people, then affiliate marketing will go hand-in-hand with your website. The more your audience trusts you, the more likely they are to follow your recommendations.

Affiliate marketing sounds good. It definitely can become a very lucrative means of income, with some bloggers earning six figures a year. However, for this method to be successful, there are a few ingredients that need to be a part of the recipe for success. These include the following:

- High website traffic

- A trusting audience

- High-quality products and services

- Products relevant to your audience

- Writing a convincing recommendation

Concerning the last ingredient, if you promote too much or too enthusiastically, you may come across as inauthentic and too pushy. People are smart enough to identify a blog that is all hype and no substance. They will notice if you are not being genuine and are just in it for the money. There needs to be a middle way, as with many things.

Creating a high-traffic website is easier than you may think. The difficulty lies in converting your visitors into customers for the companies you are affiliated. However, it can become easier if you follow these steps:

Be an expert in something. There is a lot of noise online, and there already are many experts for the major subjects out there that people are interested in. The solution to this is to necessarily become the person that people think about when they think of a topic. Find your niche and master it. Avoid being too broad with your covered subjects since that will dilute your audience. If you select one topic of focus and become an expert in it, you will find a focused and dedicated audience coming to you for insight and advice.

Promote something because you believe in it. People are usually smart enough to realize whether you genuinely believe in what you are saying about a product or whether you are just trying to sell them something to make a quick buck. Trust is the currency of the Internet, and if people trust you, they are more likely to follow your guidance on something.

Along with believing in what you are writing about, you need to provide quality content to your audience. This means that you will need to either give a very insightful commentary or research a topic extensively. If you can write an article, especially in a guide format, people will be very open to any suggestions you may have. If people find your content valuable, they may be inclined to share it on social media and further extend the reach of your affiliate links. You can include a Call to Action (CTA) in your newsletter for people to share the article with their friends and family.

In the same vein of valuable content, it is better to have fewer articles if those articles have extensive information that people can gain value from in their own lives. Quality over quantity is the key. Include a note somewhere (can be at the top of your website or blog's sidebar and the bottom of your articles) for people to subscribe to your newsletter and build up your mailing list. This will create a loyal following that will be receptive to any future affiliate products or services you may promote.

Choose the best products and services to promote. There will be affiliate products and services that will offer appealing commissions that seem very high, but if they are low-quality, it will be pointless to promote them. If you are unsure on what to promote to start, do some research in your field and see what the high-profile bloggers are promoting to generate passive income through affiliates.

You will also want to select very subject-specific products and services from affiliate marketplaces so that your audience would be interested in buying them and earning you a commission. The more targeted you are in your focus, the more likely you are to gain a more significant percentage of conversions. You might also be interested in networking with others in your field so that the extent of your reach is expanded.

If you take these steps towards setting up affiliate advertising, you will be earning passive income pretty soon. If you already have a website or blog, this is a no-brainer. You can make all your original content you have previously written work for you by giving you the financial compensation you deserve for all the time and effort you put into it. The bottom line: you will have to create meaningful and helpful value for your audience. If you do this, you will be making money while you sleep for a long time to come.

Now, we will turn to three specific methods of affiliate income, namely Google AdSense, Amazon Associates, and YouTube.

Google AdSense

Google AdSense is a Pay-Per-Click (PPC) affiliate marketing service used by over two million people and can earn you some nice passive income. AdSense will pay you when people click on an ad on your website. Some of the top bloggers use AdSense as one of the affiliate programs bringing them passive income. The amount of money you make through AdSense depends on how much money the advertisers negotiated to pay. You get paid monthly, provided that the number of clicks multiplied by the amount of money the advertisers paid for those clicks reaches the $100 threshold. The downside is if you are just starting out, it may take some time before you reach this threshold.

The content of the ads is usually quite relevant to the subject matter of the article it appears in. This will encourage your audience actually to click on the ads—that is how you will make your passive income. Google provides several different sizes for you to choose from so that the ads can seamlessly fit in with the content of your article.

One thing to note about AdSense ads is that, by default, the actual design of the ads may not go with the design of your website. Thankfully, AdSense allows you to highly customize the ads by changing the color of the text, background, border, as well as change the text size and the size of the ad boxes. You can even block certain advertisers if you feel they are not an ideal fit for the content you are sharing on your website or blog. Taking the time to tweak the ads will ensure it is worth your time to set up an AdSense account and put them on your website.

Another great feature of the AdSense platform, owned by Google, is that you get access to very insightful statistics for your website's visitors and the amount of revenue your ads are bringing in. You can even learn which articles are the most engaging with your users and how many clicks they receive. All these stats can assist you in optimizing the ads for even more passive income.

Amazon Associates

A second avenue of creating a successful stream of passive income using affiliate advertising is Amazon Associates. Like AdSense, this method of bringing in commissions has been around for a long time. There are some great reasons why you should consider Amazon Associates to bring in some passive income.

- Amazon is a reputable brand that is very safe to use. People trust Amazon and will be very likely to buy something from them when they click-through using your affiliate links.

- They pay 4% commission, which climbs up to 8% depending on the product. Since Amazon sells practically everything, receiving 4% as a start out is not that small of a commission if the product is a

4K mirrorless camera rather than a paperback book.

- People shopping on Amazon are likely to buy more than just one product. You will earn commission on anything they buy using your link, even if they do not buy the product you were initially been advertising. Since people usually buy more than one product on Amazon, the commissions can add up fast.
- Amazon offers easy-to-use tools to assist you in integrating the product links and banners into your website.

- Promoting products around the holidays is especially productive of passive income, especially on a web giant like Amazon.

While you may not earn as much passive income as with AdSense, you will still earn a very nice steady stream of income if you create informative articles such as a list of the best laptops for people on a budget or a tutorial on how to give photos a vintage look by editing them in Photoshop. Whatever it is, people love content that can help them in some way. We will now go over how to get the most out of Amazon Affiliates to make it worth your while.

The more traffic your website has, the more you will earn using Amazon Affiliates. There is a positive correlation between higher website traffic and higher affiliate commissions. If you are just beginning a new website or blog, you will find it slow-going in creating any affiliate income. If you persevere, you will continually increase your earnings over time.

Create loyal followers. If your audience consists of a sizable number of repeated visitors, this indicates that people value what you have to share and are much more likely to buy whatever it is you are promoting. Utilize the power of a mailing list to keep your audience up-to-date on your latest content.

The products you promote need to be relevant. The more relevant the products you are linking to the content of your website or blog, the more likely your audience is expected to buy them.

Create genuine reviews of products you tested. People are more inclined to buy products that someone actually tested out and was able to get the first-hand experience with. If you write a review that is as unbiased as possible, where you point out both the pros and the cons, you will more reliably generate commissions.

Promote products that are currently offered at a discount. People love a good deal or at least the semblance of one. Amazon is always selling something at a discount. If you find those products and promote them then, you could include a statement in your article about how it is 20% off right now (or whatever the deal may be).

Place product links in multiple sections of your article. Website heatmaps (they show you a map of where people move their mouse cursor on your website) have shown that, as far as affiliate links go, people click on the links when they appear below an article more than if they were elsewhere. Furthermore, people who click on the product links at the top of an article or an item bought something on Amazon (although not as often), but it was usually not the product that was linked to.

Include photos of the products you are linking to. Heatmaps have also found that people are more likely to click on affiliate links if there is an image related to the product on Amazon.

Advertise a product more than once over time. Since promoting quality over quantity is what you will be doing, you can milk the number of affiliate commissions you can receive for a particular product. Make sure to find multiple ways to talk about it over time. This is especially useful if the product is significant and something that people have been looking forward to being released for a while.

Final Thoughts

Since it takes time to build up a big enough audience where you start smiling from ear to ear about your affiliate income, start right away, and it will grow as time goes on. As you get into affiliate marketing, you will learn about it more, and you will refine your technique to fit your audience.

Also, keep the hype to a reasonable level. People want to make sure they spend their hard-earned money on something that is a quality product. If you're going to be in it for the long-term (and that is how you will make the most affiliate income), then you will want to achieve a solid reputation and maintain a loyal readership.

If you follow these tips, you will create a thorough collection of Amazon Associates links on your site that will generate long-lasting passive income that will go hand-in-hand with your Google AdSense commissions.

YouTube

While YouTube has come under some controversy lately because it has been demonetizing controversial video channels, it is still a great way to make some affiliate income. There are over a billion unique visitors to YouTube a month, and it is the second most-visited website on the Internet. Around a million people are part of the YouTube Partner Program, and some of them solely live off the passive income they receive from it.

With every 1,000 views on a monetized video, the creator can receive between $2 to $4. While it is difficult to amass 1,000,000 views on a video, it is easy to get 5,000 views per video for dozens of videos. That would all add up pretty quick if you churn out videos regularly. One thing to note is that YouTube has recently changed its rules where you will need to generate 10,000 views on your video channel before it will allow you to monetize your videos. This was put in place to reduce the number of people taking advantage of the monetizing system.

YouTube can be used to bring traffic to your website or blog. If you find yourself having trouble gaining visitors from organic search results on Google, you can create videos on YouTube to promote your site. If you already have content on your website, you can repackage it into videos. You can benefit with working less and making more if you repackage your original content in multiple ways.

You could also increase your affiliate income from Amazon Associates by speaking about products on Amazon in your videos and then putting an affiliate link into the video description. Besides reviewing products, you could create tutorial videos on how to use those products. Tutorials are very popular on YouTube and if you know how to do something, why not share your know-how?

Do you like telling stories? You can start an entire video series on YouTube where people look forward to the next episode. This is a way to build up a dedicated audience that will keep coming back for more content.

With over 100 hours of video are being uploaded to YouTube every minute, there is quite a bit of competition. For people to find your video, be sure to use the most accurate metadata. If you are not familiar with what this term means, it is just the information about your videos. This includes the title of the video, the keywords (also known as tags), and the description text of the video.

If you want to get more deeply involved in YouTube Affiliate income, become an affiliate for other companies. Plenty of companies will offer sponsorships for people that will create videos for their products and services.

The bottom line for YouTube is that you will have to create quality content to attract people to your videos. There is plenty of competition on YouTube so make sure you can make your videos stand out. If you do, you can make millions in passive income, thanks to your videos like some people are doing right now.

Chapter 4: Selling Stock Photos

Selling quality photos, you've taken to stock photo websites can be a lucrative method of passive income generation if you know how to use a nice camera. If you can get approved at one or more stock photo sites, you will be making money for years. High-quality stock photos are always sought after. You can even invest in a DSLR or a mirrorless camera and look up for tutorials online so you can become a good photographer where you could easily sell your high-quality photos as stock photos.

Perhaps you have already taken plenty of great photos which are just sitting around on your digital storage device. Why not sell them to stock photo sites? These sites will take a percentage of the sale every time one of your photos sells. You may make something like 15% per sale as a start off, but this can climb to 50% over time, especially if you exclusively sell a photo on one site that cannot be purchased anywhere else.

As with every other way to make passive income using the Internet, there is a great deal of competition so you will have to put in the effort for this method to bring in plenty of commissions. Some people live off stock photos alone, so it is definitely possible to make enough for it to send you off to beautiful and remote places in the world taking stunningly breathtaking images and sell them on stock photo sites for years and years.

Where to Sell Stock Photos

There are quite a few stock photo sites out there. Here is a list of some of the best ones that you can look over and select as marketplaces for your photos:

1. Shutterstock
2. iStock
3. PhotoDune
4. Alamy
5. Crestock
6. 123rf
7. Dreamstime
8. Corbie
9. Getty Images
10. StockXpert
11. Fotolia by Adobe
12. Bigstock Photo
13. Jupiter Images
14. Veer
15. Alaska Stock
16. Can Stock Photo

While big stock photo sites will bring you a higher rate of return as far as commissions go, their application processes are more difficult. This is why you should probably start smaller. There are over hundreds of microstock photo sites out there, so do some searches on the Internet for what would be the best fit for you. If you get rejected by some websites at the beginning of your process, do not let that dissuade you. If you take quality photos, you will eventually get approved and be on your way to making some nice passive income.

With stock photos, you will want to have a large number of images in your portfolio. Set a goal of selling 50-100 photos a month. Go even higher to 200 a month when you are starting out. If you can capture frames that are outside of the heavily-populated nature category, those will likely sell more since there is not as much competition in other areas.

When taking photos to sell to stock photo sites, be mindful that any pictures with people will have to involve signed release forms from them. You should also avoid having any recognizable brands in the pictures.

Depending on which one of these stock photo sites you choose to sell your photos on, you will receive different percentages of commissions. If you want to go the extra mile with your photos to ensure they sell well, head over to the Envato Market and hire someone to edit your photos professionally. The small initial investment in photo editing may make you quite a bit of extra money at the end of the day.

Chapter 5: Investing in REITs

Now that we have covered multiple ways to generate passive income through affiliate advertising and commissions, we will shift over to the domain of real estate. More specifically, we will look into the world of real estate investment trusts or REITs. A REIT is like a dividend you receive over time as the value of a property rises. The way this works is that the REIT invests in a property by either buying it or developing it. The trust then rents out the property or units within the property to tenants. The rent charged to the tenants is then distributed to the shareholders that are a part of the trust as a dividend.

You do not have to worry about REITs withholding the income they make, because they are legally obligated to distribute at least 90% of the taxable income they bring in. Since the money REITs make is classified as an ordinary income, they do not get double taxed like in a corporation would. They provide larger-than-normal dividends, which is appealing to investors looking for passive income. If you have a 401(k), then you may already have some investment in a REIT given that around half of all publicly-traded 401(k)s invest in a REIT.

Plenty of people have been making good money in REITs, which also means that the dividends have been declining since so many are investing in them. Nevertheless, you can still earn an excellent and consistent dividend yield.

While interest rates are low, REITs will be a worthwhile investment. However, if they go up, they may not look so appealing. The reason for this is that REITs rely on borrowed money to make their real estate acquisitions. If interest rates go up, it will cost more for them to borrow money.

REITs allow people, who would not necessarily have the money to buy real estate outright, to be able to profit from real estate. Do you have the money to buy a shopping mall? Most people don't have and, therefore, they can invest in a REIT even if they don't have the money to make such a big purchase. Even with recessions, which are a fact of life while the current fractional reserve banking system is in place, real estate is guaranteed to grow in value over the long term.

Types of REITs

There are several different kinds of REITs, although most of them specialize in one kind of property. Here is a list of the most common REITs:

- Retail – shopping centers, malls, outlets, stand-alone retail stores

- Healthcare – hospitals, nursing homes, medical buildings, senior housings

- Industrial – warehouses, factories

- Residential – apartments, some single-family homes

- Hotel – hotels, resorts, budget motels

- Self-storage – self-storage

- Data Centers – building used for data storage

All these types of REITs are good investments to bring in passive income when times are good, but what about when the inevitable recession rolls around? That is when you would want to invest in a healthcare REIT. This is called a defensive investment because they perform well no matter if the economy is doing well or not because people will always have to see doctors and go to a hospital. Furthermore, places like hospitals generally sign long-term leases, so the risk of vacancy and thereby the loss in rental income, is low.

Part of your research of which REIT to invest in should be the number of funds from operations the REIT has. The FFO is basically a REIT's earnings. The income includes an assessment of the depreciation of the assets in its holdings, plus a few other adjustments. A result is a number signifying its earnings and its ability to produce dividends. Going from there, you could use a Price/FFO multiple, so you can adequately assess the value of a REIT like you would using a Price/Earnings (P/E) ratio for stock valuation.

Choosing a Good REIT

Here are a few things to pay attention to so that you make a sound investment decision and protect yourself while searching for REITs:

Avoid new REITs. In the past few years, there are plenty of REITs that have appeared, including ones with single-family homes. Without a long track record, it is difficult to make a low-risk decision with these new REITs. It is best to see how a REIT manages different types of market conditions over time. If there are REITs that were around before the last recession, it would be helpful to look at those and also compare them to others roughly since before the recession.

Choose publicly-traded REITs. Publicly-traded REITs outperform privately-held ones over time. Also, they recover quicker after an economic downturn. Their fees are even lower than those that are not traded. When something is publicly-traded, it is required to submit its earnings report regularly, as well as other required documents. However, this sort of transparency cannot always be found in non-traded REITs, given it is not a regulatory requirement. Non-traded REITs also have to be often held for eight years or even longer.

Keep REITs a small part of your total passive income model. Sure, REITs require minimal effort on your part in generating passive income, but you should keep your entire income generation portfolio managed smartly. This means that REITs should make up around 5% to 10% of your total portfolio assets. It can be tempting to put more of your money into a high-yield REIT, but remember that no REIT is entirely risk-free. Better be safe than sorry.

If you feel ready to invest in a REIT and earn some easy passive income with no work on your part, find a broker that deals with them. There are many brokers to choose from, some of which are Fidelity, TD Ameritrade, Charles Schwab, and E*Trade. Once you go over the risks and benefits of each type of REIT and make a decision, you have the potential to earn a handsome return for a very long time.

Chapter 6: Rental Arbitrage

Do you already own a house or rented apartment, or even just an undeveloped land that you have? If not, you may want to do so after reading this because you can be making those properties work for you while you are not using them. This method of passive income creation is prevalent these days, especially with the rise of online marketplaces that allow people to rent houses, rooms, apartments, campsites, and more.

Arbitrage is basically when someone buys something at a certain price and then sells it at a higher price. With rental arbitrage, you would do something such as rent an apartment and then re-rent it on a website like Airbnb. This will bring you some easy passive income, especially if the apartment is in a popular location. You could also do this sort of rental plan using an asset you own outright, but you are less obligated with a rental, and you do not have to hold as much capital to dive into the world of rental arbitrage.

Let us look at an example of how much passive income you could generate in this way. If you sign a one-year lease on an apartment for $1,000/month and then rent it out for $2,000/month ($67/day) on Airbnb, you earn a nice $1,000 in profit. This can turn into a consistent way to make a sizable amount of passive income and is much easier to get started than if buying a property and renting it out.

There are a few different online marketplaces that have created a platform where renters and people looking to rent can match up and make a deal. The ones we will look over in greater detail are Airbnb and Hipcamp. While Airbnb deals with renting out apartments and houses, Hipcamp focuses on renting camping spots.

Airbnb

The darling of the apartment and the home-sharing economy is Airbnb. Ever since this platform cropped up, people have been able to find places to stay that were different than the same generic and bland hotels and motels we all know. If you wanted some more charm, funk, and personality, you could now go on Airbnb and find a whole array of options. It also brought people closer together in a world that has become very disconnected. If you put in a small initial investment (sign a lease on a house or apartment and furnish it), then you could be bringing in a whole lot of passive income pretty consistently for a long time to come.

The first thing you would do when exploring the option of opening up an Airbnb is to look up apartments and houses for rent. An apartment is the easier choice, but if you are intrigued by the prospect of renting out a vacation home somewhere where there are lots of outdoor activities, that would be another option. Most people stick to renting out apartments, so that will be our focus. Go on websites like Zillow and Craigslist and see what is out there for rent. Once you find something, reach out to the landlord and schedule a viewing. If you like it and agree to lease it and if you think you picked a good rental unit, then sign a one-year lease. Put up your apartment on Airbnb, get it furnished, and start seeing the bookings come.

This is the way that most people do rental arbitrage on Airbnb. However, if at some point your landlord finds out that you have been renting out their apartment without their knowledge, they may have issues with it, and you may get evicted. Fortunately, if you follow the guidelines below, you will likely be successful in having your landlord agree to you putting up the rental unit on Airbnb.

Convincing Your Landlord to Allow You to Rent Out on Airbnb

You could initially make one of four decisions:

1. Sign a lease and start renting out the apartment right away on Airbnb without telling your landlord, hoping they are alright with it if they find out

2. Sign a lease, start renting out the apartment on Airbnb, and in a few months have the conversation with your landlord about renting it out

3. Sign a lease, be a good tenant for a few months and then approach your landlord about renting the apartment on Airbnb and making a deal with them

4. Have the conversation about your plan to rent out the apartment via Airbnb while offering incentives so that you are selected as the tenant

Each of these has risks of failing depending on how your landlord feels about the situation or idea. Something else on your side might also be at risk, though, if the rental market is not that in-demand in the area. But we will focus on decision #3 since this is an approach that has a higher rate of success over the others over the long term.

For this to work, you will have to be a good tenant; you have to show the landlord that you pay on time and that you are a disciplined tenant that wouldn't cause complaints from the neighborhood. It also works better if your landlord is younger and familiar with Airbnb as well as the home-sharing economy. It also helps if the landlord doesn't own many properties. Finally, if you are the sole tenant of the apartment, that will make it easier to agree with the landlord.

If your landlord is showing hesitation in allowing you to rent out the apartment on Airbnb, you could sweeten the deal using these tactics:

- Offer to extend the lease beyond what you signed for

- Offer to pay more for the monthly rent

- Offer to share a percentage of the profit from the Airbnb rental

- Offer to purchase vacation rental insurance

- Offer to limit the times of the month and year when you rent out the unit

- Offer to revise the lease so that you cover certain damages

- Offer to increase your security deposit

- Tell them about Airbnb's $1 million insurance guarantee

- Tell them you will be only renting out rooms within the apartment and that you will be present during the stays of the guests

You should be respectful to your landlord and speak in a more casual way, so you do not come off as someone who is only looking to do business instead of forging relationships. You can explain to them that it will help you pay for your expenses and raise your quality of life. Convey to them that you can understand if it sounds risky and you are willing to make sure that it becomes advantageous for them to agree to this sort of arrangement.

If your landlord agrees, then welcome to the world of easy passive income! Now, all you have to do is furnish the apartment, set up your Airbnb profile, and put up detailed information and some appealing photos of the rental.

As far as furnishing goes, while it may seem like this will be expensive, there are ways to make it a smaller initial investment. You can order all the furnishings you would need in the Airbnb from Ikea. One of the many great things about Ikea is that they charge a flat rate for delivery. This means that you can get everything shipped to the Airbnb at once and pay a fee of around $100. If you have multiple units to rent out, you could order all the furnishings to one of them for that $100 flat rate, and then haul everything for the other units yourself to save some extra money.

While there is some effort, you will need to put into running a successful Airbnb; the amount of return you will be getting is worth it. You will need to stay on top of answering inquiries coming through the Airbnb website so that you can successfully book interested parties. You would also need to clean the unit after each party vacates it. If you would rather not do that, you could always hire an assistant to check people in and clean the unit for a reasonable fee.

Something to note: laws concerning renting out an apartment for a short-term stay differs depending on what city your apartment is located. To state an example, in New York and San Francisco, there are laws which prohibit the renting out of an apartment for less than 30 days unless the owner is around. Do some research and see what the restrictions in your area are if any. You should not have any problems in more rural areas where you may want to put up a vacation house for rent, for instance

Airbnb is a great way of bringing in passive income and having fun doing it. There are plenty of interesting people out there that you may meet—thanks to being a host—and you might make some long-lasting friendships as a result of it.

Hipcamp

Hipcamp is essentially the Airbnb of camping and glamping. These days, campsites are becoming incredibly crowded, with more people going camping than ever before. People living in the cities and suburbs looking to get away from it all can still do so on private land that the landowners charge a daily fee for.

Since the concept is very similar to Airbnb, we will only have to look at where the process differs from Airbnb. With Hipcamp, you are renting out land for people to camp on, or some dwelling that you can build or set up without any permits. These include yurts, geodesic domes, teepees, small cabins, tree houses, and micro-shelters.

Renting land is not that common of an opportunity, but you could get raw, undeveloped land at some very affordable prices in many places. Look at listing on websites such as LandWatch and reach out to the owners or realtors of the properties. Do a walk-through and get a sense if it would be a place where people could be camping out and having outdoor recreational fun. A bonus will be if there are local attractions as well.

Once you have your land set up, all you need to do is create a hosting account on the Hipcamp website, write an appealing description, and upload enticing photos. To maximize the passive income, you could bring in using Hipcamp; it would be ideal to either have a large meadow or a manicured forest grove with multiple areas cleared out for campsites so you can host various campers simultaneously, as long as they all have enough privacy.

The nice thing about choosing Hipcamp is that you don't have to be as involved as you would with an Airbnb listing, nor do you have to perform much cleaning or setting up. Some people only want a place to pitch their tent. As a renter, you would keep 90% of the revenue from any booking. As with Airbnb, they offer $1 million in liability insurance.

Besides it being a rewarding feeling knowing that you helped create life-long experiences for people in the beauty of your nature paradise, you will be earning easy passive income on land that would be underutilized in other circumstances. If you can find some affordable land somewhere, you would also get to enjoy a whole host of outdoor recreational activities whenever it is not rented out.

Chapter 7: Other Passive Income Ideas

We went over four methods of passive income generation in great depth. Now, let's take a look at six other ways to get that easy money flowing to you. These will need fewer details to get them going so they are packed into one chapter. So, here are the six other great ways to get some extra passive income:

Peer-to-Peer Lending

Peer-to-peer lending, also known as P2P lending, is simply when you loan people your money who would not usually qualify for a loan from a traditional route of lending. There are popular websites you could sign up for, such as Lending Club, Upstart, Peerform, Circleback Lending, and Prosper Marketplace, that help you get connected with people looking for a loan. The profit you can make on loan will vary from 3% to 8%. You could also take a lower-risk route using a platform such as Worth, which offers bonds and delivers you a 5% return on your investment. If at some point you need your money back, you could quickly get it back.

Create an Online Course

If you are skilled or knowledgeable about some subjects, creating a course that people could take is a fun and helpful way to bring in passive income. Your course can include e-books, support outside the course via email, and video chats. Someone can sign up for the class, and then your website can send them everything they need for the course after they pay you. If you want to take the easy route, you can create a course on a site like Teachable where most of the hard work is already taken care of for you.

Create an App

Apps, or applications, are the lifeblood of a smartphone. If you have an innovative or creative idea and know a little bit about programming, create an app. There are regular people like you making thousands of dollars a month on an app because they felt they could improve an app that already existed, or wanted to create an app for something which would make life easier in some way. If you cannot program your own app, several tools exist such as Bubble, Appery, Appy Pie, Wappler, and Thunkable, Zoho Creator, and Caspio, which will do all the coding for you. All you need to do is design the app and its functionality using an easy-to-use user interface, and voilà, you have an app!

Buy an Existing Online Business

Creating a business from the ground up can take plenty of time and resources. Why not consider buying an existing business? All the hard work has already been done for you. There are websites, such as BizBuySell, BizQuest, LoopNet, DealStream, Businesses For Sale, and Business Mart, which are essentially a marketplace selling businesses. There is a business for every price range, so take a look and see what is available and decide whether you would feel comfortable taking on an already-established online business. The way that this is a passive income generator is if you hire someone to run the business for you, so keep that in mind with this one.

Rent Out Your Car

Probably, you are not using your car, and it's just sitting in the garage most of the time. This means you are losing out on the precious passive income you could be earning while you are not using it. There are sites like HyreCar, Turo, Getaround, JustShareIt, Zimride by Enterprise, My Car Your Rental, and Fluid Market, where you can rent out your car for an average of $50 a day. You are given insurance coverage for the duration of the rental period so that you can breathe easy about your car. With Fluid Market, you can rent out a truck for people who need one to move. This is an especially lucrative way to get passive income by renting a vehicle. With a pickup, you would possibly see $12,000 a year if you rent one and double that with a box truck.

Create Licensed Audio Tracks

If you enjoy music or working with sounds, consider creating jingles or audio tracks that you can license out. Several online platforms buy audio tracks, such as TuneCore, Sonniss, Pond 5, Fantero, Audio Jingle, and iStockStudio, where you can earn credits up to 50% or more for every download or purchase of your audio creation. You will need to create a sound recording studio which could run you the cost of a good microphone and sound-proofing foam for the walls, but after that, you can record a plethora of audio tracks. Focus on audio tracks that would be appealing to people. This is easy to glean from searching for what the most popular licensed ones are. There is no harm in following in the footsteps on success.

Conclusion

Thank for making it through to the end of *11 Passive Income Secrets: How to Stop Dreaming Being Rich and Start Building Positive Cashflow*. Let's hope it was informative and able to provide you with all of the tools you need to achieve your goals.

The next step is to take what you have learned from this book and apply it to your life. Start small and simple, and go from there. If you begin to see results in something small, then you will become motivated to take on more lucrative and bold opportunities. Start somewhere. Dream big. Dwell in possibilities.

We all want to be free to work our own hours on our own terms in our private location of choice. The Internet has opened up an entirely new realm of possibilities and opportunities that have never existed before. The tools and information all exist today to achieve financial freedom from the begrudging desk jobs that so many people have, and the tedious service industry work all too many people feel stuck in. The great thing about passive income generation is that practically anyone can do it, even if it is in a small way at first. Remember, if there is anything you should doubt, it's your limit.

Finally, if you find this book useful in any way, a review on Amazon is always appreciated!

Phil C. Senior

www.ingramcontent.com/pod-product-compliance
Lightning Source LLC
Chambersburg PA
CBHW030535220526
45463CB00007B/2843

* 9 7 8 1 7 9 0 6 7 6 6 4 4 *